I0017319

# STEAM DECK OLED
# USER GUIDE

**Embarking on an ultimate gaming
journey for an immaculate display**

Valerie A. Wood

**Copyright © [2023] by [Valerie A. Wood]**

# Table of content

# Introduction

Valve Corporation's Steam Deck is a handheld gaming system that has taken the gaming community by storm. The Steam Deck, which was launched with the promise of giving a full-fledged PC gaming experience in the palm of your hand, combines the convenience of a handheld device with the power of a gaming PC.

The Steam Deck is a portable gaming console with a Zen 2 CPU and RDNA 2 GPU that works on a unique AMD APU architecture. This one-of-a-kind combination assures that the Steam Deck is more than just a gaming device, but also a little powerhouse capable of playing demanding PC games. Users can select a configuration that best suits their game library by selecting from a variety of storage capacities.

The Steam Deck's integration with the Steam platform, the largest digital distribution platform for PC games, is a noteworthy feature. This means players can access their full Steam library on the road, bringing a diverse range of games to the mobile arena, from independent gems to AAA titles.

The Steam Deck's physical design is meticulously engineered for ergonomic comfort during extended gaming sessions. The gadget has a 7-inch touchscreen display, thumbsticks, trackpads, and a full set of buttons, allowing for a diverse control scheme that appeals to a variety of game genres. The addition of gyro controllers increases the gaming possibilities even further, providing a new and engaging way to engage with games.

## The Power of an OLED Display

The Steam Deck's visual strength is centered on its OLED display, a technological marvel that takes the gaming experience to new heights. Organic Light-Emitting Diode (OLED) technology is well-known for producing vivid colors, deep blacks, and high contrast ratios.

The Steam Deck's OLED display, with a resolution of 1280 x 800, may appear modest in comparison to some flagship smartphones or high-end gaming displays, but it's the quality of the display that distinguishes it. OLED technology allows each pixel to emit its light, resulting in true blacks and contrast levels that LCDs struggle to reach.

The advantages of OLED go beyond contrast and color accuracy. The OLED display of the Steam Deck has a rapid refresh rate, ensuring smooth and fluid gameplay. This is especially important in fast-paced action games where every frame counts. The responsiveness of the display, along with the handheld form size, results in an immersive gaming experience that is difficult to match.

Furthermore, OLED technology promotes HDR (High Dynamic Range), which improves the visual spectrum and provides a more lifelike portrayal of colors. This is especially noticeable in games that use HDR to produce spectacular images and realistic lighting effects. The OLED display on the Steam Deck serves as a canvas for game creators to showcase their ideas with astounding fidelity.

The OLED display improves multimedia consumption on the Steam Deck in addition to gaming. Users can expect brilliant and true-to-life visuals that make any type of entertainment on this handheld device a pleasure, whether viewing movies, browsing photos, or enjoying other non-gaming content.

The Steam Deck's OLED display is more than simply a technological feature; it's a portal to a visually spectacular gaming universe. The Steam Deck is a tempting alternative for gamers looking for a great gaming experience in a portable package thanks to its cutting-edge hardware, intelligent design, and the power of OLED technology. As we go deeper into the OLED User Guide, we'll look at how to unlock the full potential of this magnificent display for an unforgettable gaming experience.

*Let's get started*

# Chapter 1: Getting Started

The thrill of opening a new game system is unparalleled, and the Steam Deck is no exception. Setting up your Steam Deck is a simple step that ensures you're ready to jump right into the gaming world.

## Installing Your Steam Deck

Begin by unpacking your Steam Deck and its accessories with care. You'll find the console, power adapter, USB-C cable, and any extras you ordered. To ensure an uninterrupted gaming experience, charge the smartphone completely before turning it on.

To turn on your Steam Deck, press and hold the power button on the device's top. Select your language, region, and other basic preferences by following the on-screen prompts. Connecting to Wi-Fi is a necessary step in order to access the most recent updates, game downloads, and online features. Navigate to the Wi-Fi settings menu and enter your network credentials.

Once connected, the Steam Deck will prompt you to sign in or create a new Steam account. You may access your game collection, achievements, and other personalized features by signing in. If you don't already have a Steam account, the setup wizard will walk you through the process of creating one.

## *Configuration of the First OLED Display*

Now that your Steam Deck is turned on and connected, you can adjust the OLED display settings for the best visual experience. Navigate to the display settings menu, where you may change the brightness, contrast, and resolution. The Steam Deck's OLED display features brilliant colors and deep blacks, creating a spectacular visual canvas for your games.

Experiment with various display configurations to find the settings that work best for you. When altering brightness and contrast, consider factors such as ambient lighting and personal comfort. Higher resolution settings can improve image quality, but they must be balanced against performance, especially in resource-intensive games.

The OLED display on the Steam Deck supports dynamic HDR, which enhances the gaming experience with lifelike colors and enhanced contrast. Explore the HDR settings and enable this option to experience more realistic games. Keep in mind that not all games may support HDR, therefore verify compatibility with individual game settings.

## Tips for Calibration and Setup

Calibrating the OLED display on your Steam Deck ensures correct color representation and optimal performance. Color temperature, gamma, and other advanced variables are adjusted throughout the calibration process. Although the device comes with pre-set calibration profiles, fine-tuning them to your tastes can improve visual quality even further.

Consider using external calibration instruments or checking online resources for recommended settings for proper calibration. Some people prefer warmer or cooler color tones, and the adaptability of

OLED technology allows you to customize the display to your preferences.

If available, look into advanced features like motion blur reduction and adaptive sync. These improvements improve gameplay by eliminating motion blur and screen tearing. Adjust the parameters to meet the individual needs of the games you play.

Unboxing, powering up, and setting the OLED display for an immersive gaming experience are all part of the initial setup of your Steam Deck. Take your time exploring the many options, customizing them to your liking, and get ready to begin an exciting voyage through the world of gaming with the enhanced visuals provided by your Steam Deck's OLED display.

# Chapter 2: Navigating the OLED Interface

The Steam Deck, with its brilliant OLED display, provides customers with an immersive interface that improves the game experience. In this section, we'll go over how to navigate the OLED interface, including the Steam Deck Menu System, Gesture Controls, and Accessing Display Settings.

## System of Steam Deck Menus

The Menu System, located at the heart of the Steam Deck's interface, provides access to a wealth of gaming choices and settings. When you turn on your device, the menu appears, revealing a graphically rich and dynamic hub for all of your gaming pursuits.

The Menu System is user-friendly, with straightforward categorizations that make it simple to access games, programs, and system settings. Users may easily traverse their library, explore recent activity, and discover new titles.

One notable feature is the use of dynamic previews within the menu tiles. When you hover your mouse over a game or application, a fragment of its content or action is presented, giving you a preview before you plunge in. This not only improves the interface's visual attractiveness but also aids in faster decision-making, especially when you're spoiled for choice in your huge game library.

The Menu System is dynamic and changes based on your usage patterns. Games and programs that are frequently accessed take center stage, ensuring that your favorites are always within reach. The clever learning algorithms in Steam Deck adapt to your preferences, providing a personalized and dynamic user experience.

Users can experiment with customizing choices to get the most out of the Steam Deck Menu System. Customizing the tile layout, establishing folders for specific genres, and pinning favorite titles to the home screen are just a few ways to customize the interface. This amount of adaptability allows players to customize their gaming environment based on their tastes.

## Navigation and Gesture Controls

Gesture controls bring the Steam Deck interface to a whole new level of involvement. Intuitive motions offer a tactile dimension to your interactions, whether you're navigating the menu or immersed in games.

Swiping between menu tiles, pinch-to-zoom for detailed views, and gesture shortcuts for quick access to certain functions all help to provide a smooth and responsive navigation experience. These movements are intended to be intuitive, decreasing the learning curve and improving overall interface accessibility.

In-game motions are also important. Consider altering settings or accessing in-game menus with a simple swipe or tap that is flawlessly integrated and does not interrupt your gaming flow. Gesture controls on the Steam Deck are more than just a curiosity; they are a functional improvement that adds a touch of class to your gaming interactions.

Users can tailor the gesture settings to their tastes. Whether you like subtle gestures or more apparent movements, the choice is entirely yours. This customization ensures that the gesture controls improve, rather than detract from, your overall game experience.

## *Changing Display Options*

The beauty of the OLED display is found not only in its visual brilliance but also in the control it provides users. Accessing Display Settings on the Steam Deck allows you to personalize the display, ensuring that the visual experience matches your tastes.

Users can fine-tune characteristics like as brightness, contrast, and color saturation in the Display Settings. Whether you like a bright and colorful display for action-packed games or a more subdued tone for dramatic experiences, the customization options allow you to build your ideal visual environment.

Resolution and refresh rate adjustments also help to optimize your gaming graphics. The OLED display of the Steam Deck supports high resolutions, delivering clear and detailed graphics. By adjusting these options, users can find a compromise between visual fidelity and performance, responding to personal preferences and game needs.

The Steam Deck's Display Settings include advanced features in addition to simple display settings. HDR calibration, color temperature changes, and gamma settings give both casual gamers and display experts a level of control. Exploring these advanced settings reveals a plethora of options for personalizing the display to various genres, emotions, or even times of day.

Navigating the OLED interface on the Steam Deck is more than just moving between menus; it's also about shaping your game experience. The Menu System, Gesture Controls, and Display Settings all work together to provide a comprehensive and customized experience, guaranteeing that the OLED display becomes a blank canvas for your gaming masterpieces. As you play games with the Steam Deck, these aspects work together to reveal the full power of the OLED interface and turn every interaction into a visual treat.

# Chapter 3: Optimizing Display Settings for Gaming

Gaming has developed into a visually engaging experience, and the OLED display on the Steam Deck provides a canvas for exceptional graphics. To achieve the highest visual fidelity, fine-tuning the display settings becomes critical. This section will go over three important topics: fine-tuning resolution and refresh rate, HDR and color calibration, and implementing best practices for game-specific settings.

## *Adjusting the Resolution and Refresh Rate*

Your gaming experience is greatly influenced by the resolution and refresh rate of your Steam Deck's OLED display. It is critical to strike the correct balance between clarity and performance.

Begin by investigating your game's native resolution. Changing the resolution guarantees a clear image without sacrificing performance. Because the high pixel density of the OLED display enables intricate features to shine, finding the sweet spot that corresponds with your preferences and the capabilities of your device is critical.

The refresh rate is also critical for achieving seamless gameplay. The Steam Deck offers a variety of refresh rates, and choosing the best one can dramatically improve motion smoothness. Higher refresh rates, such as

120Hz or 144Hz, can make gaming more responsive and immersive.

Experiment with different resolution and refresh rate combinations based on the requirements of the games you play. A greater refresh rate may benefit competitive gaming, whereas a higher resolution may highlight visual integrity in narrative-driven games.

## High Dynamic Range and Color Calibration

The richness and realism of graphics on the OLED display are enhanced by High Dynamic Range (HDR) and color calibration. HDR broadens the luminance and color ranges, allowing for a more genuine portrayal of scenes.

Begin by enabling HDR in the system settings, then fine-tune it to meet the individual needs of each game. Many recent games support HDR, and tweaking the in-game HDR settings provides appropriate balance and avoids overly saturated or washed-out colors.

Color calibration entails reproducing accurate colors on the OLED screen. The Steam Deck allows you to change the color temperature, saturation, and hue. Adjust these parameters to reflect your personal preferences as well as the artistic aim of the games you play. A well-calibrated display not only improves visual appeal but also ensures that each game's intended ambiance is effectively portrayed.

## Game-Specific Settings Best Practices

Every game is distinct, and customizing display settings for each title can improve the gaming experience. Consider the excellent practices listed below:

- **Profiles and Presets**:
Many games have pre-configured graphical settings or allow you to create custom profiles. Experiment with these variables to get the right combination of performance and visual quality for you.

- **In-Game Modifications**:
For more customization, go to the in-game graphical settings menu. Changing factors like as texture quality, shadows, and anti-aliasing can have a big impact on the appearance.

- **Performance Evaluation:**
While adjusting parameters, keep an eye on performance data. Steam Deck has tools for monitoring frame rates and assessing the impact of modifications on performance in real-time.

- **Recommendations from the Community**:

Gaming communities frequently provide the best settings for individual titles. Using these insights will help you save time and achieve the best combination of looks and performance.

Optimizing display settings for gaming on the Steam Deck's OLED panel requires a careful balance of resolution, refresh rate, HDR, and color calibration. Customizing these settings to each game's specific qualities offers a visually spectacular and responsive gaming experience, allowing you to fully immerse yourself in the digital worlds that await.

# Chapter 4: Understanding OLED Technology on Steam Deck

OLED, or Organic Light-Emitting Diode, technology has revolutionized display technology and has found its way into a variety of electrical gadgets, including the Steam Deck. In this in-depth look, we'll look at the complexities of OLED display technology, its benefits, unique features, and the transformative impact it has on the gaming experience.

## An In-Depth Look at OLED Display Technology

A unique organic chemical at the heart of OLED technology generates light when an electric current is applied. OLED displays, unlike typical LED or LCDs, do not require a backlight. Because of this basic distinction, each pixel can generate its light independently, providing unmatched control over brightness and contrast.

The organic layers in OLED displays are made up of carbon-based chemicals, therefore the name "organic." When an electric current travels through these layers placed between two electrodes, it triggers the organic molecules to generate light. This self-emitting feature is essential for OLEDs to produce genuine black levels and bright hues.

One distinguishing element of OLED technology is its adaptability. OLED displays can be produced on flexible substrates, allowing for curved or even folding screens. Although this flexibility provides a layer of innovation and design freedom, it may not be fully utilized in the context of a gaming device such as the Steam Deck.

However, OLED panels are not without their difficulties. Concerns have been expressed about the potential for burn-in or uneven pixel degradation over time. To address these challenges, manufacturers have developed various technologies like pixel shifting and screen savers. Understanding the technology is necessary for users to make informed decisions regarding usage patterns and display settings to extend the life of their OLED screens.

## *Benefits and Distinctive Features*

OLED technology has various advantages, making it a popular choice for premium displays:

- **Excellent Black Levels**:
Because OLED pixels can be turned off individually, full black levels are achieved, improving contrast and delivering a more immersive visual experience.

- **Quick Reaction Time**:
When compared to typical LCD panels, OLED displays feature faster response times, which reduces motion blur and ghosting in fast-paced gaming conditions.

- **Extensive Viewing Angles**:
OLEDs have outstanding viewing angles with constant colors even at extreme angles, delivering a fascinating experience for multiplayer gaming or sharing content.

- **Extremely Fast Refresh Rates**:

Many OLED screens, including the Steam Deck's, have high refresh rates, which contribute to smoother gameplay and better responsiveness.

- **Lightweight and Thin**:
OLED screens are tiny and lightweight by nature, which contributes to the overall portability and sleek appearance of products like the Steam Deck.

Understanding these benefits helps users understand why OLED technology is an attractive alternative for gaming fans looking for a superior visual experience.

## How OLED Improves the Gaming Experience

The incorporation of OLED technology into the Steam Deck transforms the game experience, raising visuals to new heights:

- **Vibrant Colors and High Dynamic Range:**

The ability of OLED to display pure black improves dynamic range, allowing for more bright and lifelike colors. High Dynamic Range (HDR) support enhances the visual experience by giving a broader color range and enhanced contrast.

- **Intense Contrast:**

A more immersive gaming environment is created by the combination of excellent black depths and high contrast ratios. Details in shadows and highlights become more prominent, boosting the images' overall depth and realism.

- **Sensitive Gameplay**:

OLED displays' rapid response time eliminates input lag and motion blur, resulting in a more responsive and fluid gaming experience. This is especially important in genres where split-second reactions can make a big difference.

- **Personalization and customization**:

Because of OLED's pixel control, it is possible to precisely customize lighting effects and images in games that support it. This functionality can be used by developers to create unique atmospheres and enrich the gaming story.

OLED technology on the Steam Deck goes above typical display capabilities, providing gamers with a visual feast of bright colors, deep blacks, and greater responsiveness. Understanding the technology enables players to get the most out of their gaming experience while also taking the necessary safeguards to protect the longevity of their OLED displays. OLED is at the vanguard of technological advancement, altering how we view and engage with digital entertainment.

# Chapter 5: Customizing OLED Display for Your Preferences

Customizing your Steam Deck's OLED display goes beyond plain functionality; it's about building an immersive and personalized gaming experience tailored to your preferences. In this section, we'll delve into the complexities of tailoring your Steam Deck, focusing on three major aspects: personalizing the home screen and themes, establishing custom display profiles, and integrating external customization tools.

## *Customizing the Home Screen and Themes*

Personalizing your Steam Deck's home screen acts as the portal to your gaming universe, and it adds a touch of personality. Begin by looking through the theme options, where you may select from a number of pre-installed themes or make your own. Choose colors, backgrounds, and icons that complement your gaming style. Whether you choose a sleek, minimalist design or colorful, dynamic images, the Steam Deck's OLED display serves as a blank canvas for your imagination.

Consider personalizing app icons to help you quickly identify your favorite games or apps. Assigning distinct wallpapers to various game categories can help improve organization and visual attractiveness. Explore the settings menu for extensive customization options like altering icon sizes and grid layouts to optimize the home screen for easy navigation.

## *Creating Individual Display Profiles*

A true gaming expert would tailor display settings to match the intricacies of each game. Steam Deck allows you to create custom display profiles that ensure each title is shown in its best visual light. Begin by going to the display settings menu and choosing the option to create a new profile.

Fine-tune characteristics such as brightness, contrast, and color saturation based on the needs of each game. In a dark and moody adventure, for example, you may want more contrast and lower brightness to accentuate shadows and enhance immersion. Adjusting color saturation, on the other hand, helps bring out the richness of in-game images in brilliant and colorful games.

Save and name each profile according to the game, resulting in a library of personalized settings ready to improve your gaming experience. The seamless transition between profiles guarantees that your Steam Deck reacts to the specific qualities of each title, giving unrivaled visual accuracy.

## Including Third-Party Customization Tools

Extend your customization quest by investigating external tools that supplement the Steam Deck's innate possibilities. External customization tools, which are frequently created by the gaming community, can provide further features and fine-grained control over display settings.

Before integrating external tools, make sure they are compatible with the firmware version of your Steam Deck. These tools may include advanced options for fine-tuning color accuracy, gamma settings, and even the creation of new shaders for a totally customized visual experience.

Participate in online groups to learn about popular customizing tools and to share your knowledge with other gamers. Keep in mind that, while external tools can enable new levels of customization, they must be used wisely and with consideration for any potential influence on system stability.

Personalizing the OLED display on your Steam Deck is an exercise in self-expression and optimization. The Steam Deck lets you personalize your gaming environment, from creating visually attractive home screens to customizing display profiles for each game. Integrating external customization tools provides an additional degree of versatility, allowing you to push the limits of visual modification. Accept the limitless possibilities that the OLED display provides, and start on a gaming trip where every pixel reflects your distinct style and tastes.

# Chapter 6: Managing Power Consumption with OLED Features

As gamers immerse themselves in the immersive world of the Steam Deck's OLED display, it becomes increasingly important to achieve a balance between appealing visuals and effective power management. In this section, we'll look at how to manage power consumption with OLED features, including power-saving choices, altering brightness and contrast, and understanding how OLED settings affect battery life.

## *OLED Power-Saving Options*

Because of their ability to individually regulate each pixel, OLED displays have a distinct edge in terms of power efficiency. Steam Deck offers a variety of power-saving features optimized for the OLED display to enhance power savings. Typical alternatives include:

- **Refresh Rates Dynamic**:

The refresh rate of the Steam Deck's OLED display can be dynamically adjusted depending on the content displayed. Lower refresh rates in static or less demanding scenes contribute to significant power savings while maintaining the gaming experience.

- **Pixel Dimming**:

OLED's pixel-level control allows for exact pixel dimming. This feature is useful in situations when deep blacks are prominent since pixels can be turned off completely, conserving power and improving contrast ratios.

- **Optimization of Sleep Mode**:

When the device is not in use, Steam Deck handles the OLED display smartly by entering low-power sleep modes. This guarantees that power consumption is kept to a minimum during inactivity while retaining speedy responsiveness when the device is re-engaged.

- **Adaptive Lighting**:

Steam Deck frequently incorporates ambient light sensors, which alter the brightness of the display depending on its surroundings. This not only improves user comfort but also helps to save energy by regulating brightness levels based on external illumination conditions.

## *Changing the Brightness and Contrast*

The ability to fine-tune the brightness and contrast settings on the OLED display is critical for battery management. Users have extensive control over these factors with Steam Deck, allowing for a tailored gaming experience while optimizing power consumption.

- **Calibration of Brightness**:
Users can adjust the brightness level manually to suit their preferences and the environment. Finding the proper mix delivers a great viewing experience while minimizing battery strain.

- **Contrast Enhancement**:
The ability of OLEDs to produce true black levels adds to their excellent contrast ratios. Users can adjust the contrast levels to

improve vision in low-light situations while keeping power consumption in mind.

- **Professional Gaming Profiles**:
Steam Deck frequently includes pre-set gaming settings that alter brightness and contrast based on the type of game being played. This not only improves the gaming experience but also aids in energy efficiency by adjusting settings to specific content.

- **Battery Life Impact of OLED Settings**

Understanding how OLED settings affect battery life is critical for those looking to get the most out of their Steam Deck gaming experiences. While OLED provides unsurpassed visuals, users can employ ways to balance visual fidelity with extended battery life.

- **Optimal Extended Play Settings**:

Users can considerably lengthen their gaming sessions without sacrificing the overall visual experience by taking a balanced approach to brightness, contrast, and refresh rates. Experimenting with various settings and determining the sweet spot for individual preferences is critical.

- **Battery Monitoring in Real Time**: Steam Deck frequently includes real-time battery monitoring capabilities that show current power consumption based on OLED settings. This feature allows customers to make informed decisions by allowing them to alter settings on the fly to achieve the optimal mix of performance and battery life.

- **Presets for Battery Life**: Some Steam Deck models may include established battery life presets, letting players choose between optimum settings for longer bursts of play and maximum graphic fidelity for shorter bursts. These presets make it easier to manage OLED settings based on the length of gaming sessions.

The OLED display on the Steam Deck adds a new level to portable gaming, and good power management is critical for an excellent experience. Users may tailor their OLED experience to find the perfect mix of exciting images and extended gameplay by exploiting power-saving tools, tweaking brightness and contrast settings, and understanding the impact on battery life. The deliberate integration of OLED technologies in the Steam Deck allows customers to embark on an ultimate gaming journey while extending the life of their portable gaming device.

# Chapter 7: Troubleshooting OLED Display Issues

The OLED panels on the Steam Deck provide an immersive gaming experience, but like any technology, they are not without flaws. In this section, we'll look at frequent OLED display issues, the need for firmware updates, and how to get advanced help when necessary.

## *Typical Display Issues and Solutions*

❖ **Problem 1: Screen Burn-in**

**Description**:
Burn-in can occur when there are persistent images on the screen.

### → **Solution**:
Turn on features such as pixel shifting, screensavers, and periodic screen darkening. Avoid leaving static graphics on the screen for long periods.

### ❖ **Problem 2:**
**Dead Pixels**

**Description**:
Individual pixels may fail to display, resulting in the appearance of little black spots.

### → **Action**:
During the first setup, check for dead pixels. If a defect is discovered, examine the device's warranty or contact support for a possible replacement.

## ❖ Problem 3: Color Irregularities

**Description**:
 Colors that are inaccurate or have uneven brightness across the screen.

### → Solution:
In the display menu, adjust the color calibration settings. If the problem persists, consider using professional calibrating tools.

## ❖ Problem 4: Flickering or Screen Fluctuations

**Description**:
Intermittent flickering or abrupt brightness shifts.

### → Action:
Check that the device's firmware is up to date. Adjust the refresh rate of the monitor

and try alternative connectors if it is connected to an external display.

## ❖ Problem 5:
## Image Retention

**Description**:
  The temporary retention of previously displayed images on the screen.

## → Solution:
To avoid image retention, use screen refresh features. If the problem persists, consider decreasing the screen brightness or contacting support.

## *Firmware Updates for Display Issues*

Firmware updates are critical for ensuring optimal OLED display performance. Manufacturers issue updates regularly to resolve bugs, improve stability, and introduce new features. Here are some of the reasons why staying current is critical:

## Importance of Firmware Updates:

- **Bug Fixes**:
Patches for recognized display faults, such as flickering, color inconsistencies, or unexpected behavior, are frequently included in updates.

- **Optimization**:
Through updates, manufacturers fine-tune OLED performance, improving overall display quality and responsiveness.

- **Security**:
Firmware updates may contain security fixes that protect your device from potential vulnerabilities.

## Check for Updates:
- Update Firmware:Navigate to your Steam Deck's system settings. To

check for the most recent firmware, go for the "Software" or "System Update" area.

- Follow these steps: If a firmware update is available, follow the on-screen instructions to download and install it.
- Data Backup: It is recommended that you backup your data before doing firmware updates to avoid data loss in the event of unanticipated complications.

## Manual vs. Automatic Updates:

- Manual Updates: Some gadgets allow you to enable automatic updates. Consider using this feature if it is available to ensure that your device is always running the most recent firmware.
- Manual Updating: If automatic updates are not available, check for

firmware updates and install them manually regularly.

## Requesting Advanced Assistance from Support

Despite the availability of self-help methods, there are times when professional aid is required. If you are experiencing chronic display issues or are confused about implementing remedies, contacting assistance can be beneficial.

### When Should You Contact Support?

- Recurring Issues: If difficulties persist despite standard troubleshooting procedures, it's time to seek professional help.
- Hardware Concerns: Contacting support for hardware evaluation is recommended for issues such as dead pixels, screen burn-in, or physical damage.

- Firmware Issues: If you have problems throughout the firmware update process or think that you have a firmware-related problem, support can walk you through the procedure or give alternate solutions.

## Getting Ready for Support Contact:

- Documentation: Write down precise details regarding the problem, such as when it began, how frequently it occurs, and any error messages.
- System Information: Provide important system information, such as firmware and software versions, as well as any recent device changes.
- Warranty Details: If the equipment is still under warranty, keep the warranty information on hand. Some problems may be covered by insurance for replacement or repair.

## Contact Methods:

- Online Help Portals: Many manufacturers have online support portals where customers can submit tickets or interact with representatives via live chat.
- Phone Assistance: Consider phoning the device manufacturer's support hotline if the problem requires quick attention.

proactively troubleshooting and keeping your device's firmware up to date are critical to maintaining a fluid OLED display experience on your Steam Deck. If difficulties continue, do not hesitate to contact support for experienced advice in making the most of your gaming experience.

# Chapter 8: Enhancing Gaming Experience with OLED

The introduction of OLED display technology has been a major changer in the area of gaming, where visuals are critical to immersion. With its brilliant OLED screen, the Steam Deck elevates gaming experiences to new heights. In this investigation, we go into the aspects of how OLED improves gaming, demonstrating its impact on graphics and providing recommendations for titles that truly shine on an OLED panel.

## *OLED Immersive Gaming*

The capacity of OLED, or Organic Light-Emitting Diode, technology to offer deep blacks, bright colors, and high contrast ratios is recognized. These elements substantially contribute to the creation of an immersive gaming environment. OLED pixels, unlike typical LCD pixels, emit their own light, allowing for pixel-level control. This implies that in dark scenes, pixels can be totally turned off, resulting in true blacks and no backlight bleed.

Consider exploring a poorly lit dungeon in a role-playing game or feeling the suspense of a horror title; OLED's ability to reproduce true blacks gives an unprecedented depth to shadows and atmospheres. The contrast between light and dark becomes more pronounced, heightening the overall gaming atmosphere and increasing the intensity of each moment.

Furthermore, the high response time of OLED means that fast-paced action sequences are portrayed with exceptional clarity, minimizing motion blur. This functionality is especially useful in genres such as first-person shooters and racing games, where quick reactions can make or break the game.

## Demonstrating the Impact of OLED on Graphics

Graphics are an essential component of the gaming experience, and OLED displays excel at bringing visual material to life. OLED screens' brilliant and true-to-life colors add to the depth of in-game scenes. Every detail, from gorgeous landscapes to futuristic cityscapes, is rendered with a level of realism that captivates the player.

OLED's high dynamic range (HDR) features offer even more to the visual spectacle. HDR broadens the color and brightness ranges available, allowing for a more nuanced and realistic representation of lighting conditions. Sunsets become more spectacular, and water reflections more convincing, immersing players in a visually magnificent world.

Aside from color accuracy, the high refresh rates of OLED contribute to better images and animations. Games feel more responsive, and motion fluidity improves the overall gaming experience. Whether you're exploring open-world landscapes or engaging in fierce battle, OLED's graphic rendering capability ensures that every frame is a visual feast.

## OLED Display Recommended Games

Certain games are designed with visual characteristics that benefit greatly from OLED panels. Here are some suggestions for fully utilizing the possibilities of your Steam Deck's OLED screen:

- **Horror Movie Titles**:
Games that rely on atmospheric tension and dark locales, such as "Resident Evil Village" or "Amnesia: Rebirth," are enhanced on OLED panels, heightening the spine-chilling experience.

- **Adventures in an Open World:**
Titles such as "The Legend of Zelda: Breath of the Wild" and "Red Dead Redemption 2" have huge vistas and rich features that pop on OLED screens, making for a breathtaking voyage through virtual worlds.

- **Games with High Dynamic Range**:

Use HDR capabilities in games like "Cyberpunk 2077" or "Final Fantasy XV," where the dynamic range improves the realism and depth of the visuals.

- **Action Games with a Fast Pace**: Games like "Call of Duty: Warzone" and "Doom Eternal" benefit from OLED's fast response times, which ensure that every movement is depicted precisely and clearly.

The OLED display on the Steam Deck converts gaming into a visually attractive and immersive experience. OLED technology increases the visual components of gaming, from the depth of blacks to the richness of colors, making it an important component for those seeking the ideal gaming journey.

As you travel through various virtual worlds, the OLED display acts as a portal, bringing every pixel to life in a way that genuinely reflects the genius of game makers.

# Chapter 9: Exploring Additional Features of Steam Deck's OLED Screen

The Steam Deck, with its bright OLED screen, goes beyond gaming to provide a diverse entertainment experience. Aside from gaming, this portable powerhouse introduces a slew of features that take advantage of the advantages of its OLED display, transforming it into a multipurpose multimedia device.

## *Multimedia and OLED Beyond Gaming*

The Steam Deck's OLED screen is more than just a gaming canvas; it's a portal to a world of multimedia possibilities. The Steam Deck's OLED display amplifies every pixel for a compelling experience, whether you're a movie lover, music enthusiast, or simply enjoy streaming your favorite material.

Imagine being able to immerse yourself in the rich colors and deep blacks of your favorite movies while on the road. Because of the OLED's ability to independently illuminate pixels, it achieves true blacks and a contrast ratio that brings cinematic scenes to life. The OLED display enhances the visual quality of your multimedia consumption, from colorful animations to fine details in gloomy movie moments.

With the OLED's color accuracy and vibrancy, music takes on a new dimension. The album artwork is vibrant, and the dynamic spectrum of colors adds a new dimension to the whole listening experience.

Whether you're watching a music video or scrolling through your favorite playlist, the OLED display makes the visual accompaniment as immersive as the audio.

## OLED Integration with Steam Features

The incorporation of OLED into Steam features brings up a whole new universe of possibilities for both gamers and content providers. Steam's Big Picture mode, which is meant for large displays, smoothly adjusts to the OLED screen on the Steam Deck, delivering an easy and visually appealing interface for browsing and purchasing games.

Each game cover is presented with remarkable clarity and depth, making browsing through your game library a visual feast. The fast refresh rate of the OLED enables smooth transitions, resulting in a compelling user experience. The OLED integration in Steam Deck extends to in-game overlays, letting you use Steam's social services without disturbing your gaming experience.

Furthermore, the OLED on the Steam Deck improves the streaming experience for people who enjoy broadcasting their gameplay. The OLED display ensures that every frame is presented with clarity and vibrancy, increasing the visual quality of your streams whether you're demonstrating your skills or creating content for your audience.

## OLED Interface's Hidden Gems

Beyond the apparent advantages, the OLED interface contains hidden jewels that consumers may not discover at first. Customization capabilities, such as personalized backgrounds and themes, enable users to tailor the OLED display to their tastes, resulting in a distinctive and visually appealing experience.

Furthermore, the responsiveness of the OLED extends to touch controllers, adding an extra degree of interaction. This functionality isn't just for games; it improves the general user experience, making navigation faster and more natural. The responsiveness of the OLED provides a tactile element to your contact with the Steam Deck, whether you're exploring your multimedia library or tweaking settings.

The exploration of new functionality on the Steam Deck's OLED screen extends beyond games. It turns the gadget into a multimedia powerhouse, enhancing the visual experience of movies, music, and other media. The incorporation of OLED with Steam features expands gaming and content creation opportunities, while hidden jewels within the OLED interface allow users to personalize and enhance their entire experience. The OLED screen on the Steam Deck is more than simply a monitor; it's a portal to a world of bright, immersive, and personalized entertainment.

# Chapter 10: Safety Tips for Using OLED Display

Long-term use of OLED panels, such as the one on the Steam Deck, necessitates careful attention to maintain both optimal performance and user comfort. OLED technology, which is noted for its brilliant colors and excellent contrast, necessitates special considerations for long-term use.

When engaging in extended gaming sessions or using the display for an extended period, users should keep the following principles in mind:

- **Screen Dimming and Burn-In Prevention**:

OLED displays are prone to burn-in, which occurs when static images are displayed for an extended period and cause irreparable damage. Consider enabling screen dimming or screen savers during inactive periods to avoid this danger.

- **Content Rotation:**
Rotate the content on the screen regularly to prevent uneven wear on certain pixels. Games and applications containing static features, such as health bars or maps, should be rotated regularly to spread wear equally.

- **Brightness Levels:**
Adapt the brightness settings to the lighting circumstances. Excessive brightness not only affects power usage but can also cause eye strain when used over extended periods.

- **Scheduled Breaks**:
Incorporate breaks into long gaming or display usage periods. Taking short breaks

not only alleviates eye strain but also allows the OLED pixels to refresh, lowering the chance of burn-in.

- **Update Firmware**:
Check for firmware upgrades offered by the device maker regularly. These updates may feature optimizations and improvements that help the OLED display last longer.

- **Cooling Considerations**:
Ensure sufficient ventilation and cooling for the device, as OLED displays can generate heat when used for an extended period. Overheating may have an impact not only on display performance but also on the device's overall longevity.

## *Cleaning and Upkeep*

Keeping the OLED display clean is critical for keeping visual quality and avoiding potential problems. Here are some pointers for cleaning and maintaining your OLED screen:

- **Microfiber Cloth:**
For regular cleaning, use a soft, lint-free microfiber cloth. This sort of material reduces the possibility of screen scratches.

- **Avoid Harmful Chemicals**:
On the OLED display, do not use abrasive cleaners, solvents, or strong chemicals. These substances can harm the protective coatings and impair the functionality of the display.

- **Turn Off the Device**:
Before cleaning the screen, turn off the Steam Deck or any other electrical device. This prevents functionalities from being accidentally activated during the cleaning process.

- **Gentle Wiping Motion:**

Use a gentle wiping motion when cleaning. Apply light pressure to avoid damaging the screen or its covering.

- **Pay Special Attention to the Edges and Corners:**

Pay special attention to the OLED display's edges and corners, as these regions can accumulate dust and debris.

- **Protective Covers**:

Consider utilizing an OLED-specific protective cover or screen protector. These accessories can provide an additional layer of protection against scratches and mild abrasions.

## OLED Health Considerations

While OLED screens provide amazing visual experiences, users should be aware of the potential health risks connected with prolonged screen exposure:

- **Eye Strain**:
Take frequent pauses to avoid eye strain. Prolonged gaming or screen time without breaks can cause discomfort, exhaustion, and other eye problems.

- **Blue Light Emission**:
OLED screens generate blue light, which may interfere with sleep. Consider utilizing "night mode" settings or blue light filters, particularly in the evening.

- **Ergonomic Gaming Setup**:
Keep an ergonomic gaming setup to reduce physical strain. To promote comfort during long sessions, place the display at eye level, utilize an adjustable chair, and guarantee optimal hand positioning.

- **Room Lighting:**
Adequate ambient lighting in the room aids in the reduction of eye strain. Adjust the

lighting conditions to avoid excessive glare on the screen.

- **Adjustable Display Settings:**
Experiment with and personalize display settings like brightness and color temperature to fit personal comfort preferences and reduce eye strain.

Finally, adhering to these instructions for extended usage, cleaning, and health considerations guarantees that users may enjoy the benefits of the OLED display on the Steam Deck while maintaining both the display's performance and well-being.

www.ingramcontent.com/pod-product-compliance
Lightning Source LLC
LaVergne TN
LVHW051608050326
832903LV00033B/4404